James O Blakeley

An Outline Harmony of the Gospels

And Key to an Outline Chart of the Journeyings, Principal Events and....

James O Blakeley

An Outline Harmony of the Gospels
And Key to an Outline Chart of the Journeyings, Principal Events and....

ISBN/EAN: 9783337211301

Printed in Europe, USA, Canada, Australia, Japan

Cover: Foto ©Lupo / pixelio.de

More available books at **www.hansebooks.com**

An Outline
Harmony of the Gospels

—AND—

KEY TO AN OUTLINE CHART

- OF—

The Journeyings, Principal Events
and Teachings

—IN THE—

LIFE OF JESUS—THE CHRIST

— — —

1896
JAMES O. BLAKELEY
LOS ANGELES, CAL.

An Outline
Harmony of the Gospels

—AND—

KEY TO AN OUTLINE CHART

—OF—

The Journeyings, Principal Events and Teachings

—IN THE—

Life of Jesus—The Christ

—OR—

THE HISTORICAL CONTENTS OF MATTHEW, MARK,
LUKE AND JOHN COMPARED, CLASSIFIED AND
CHARACTERIZED WITH ESPECIAL REFERENCE
TO THE PROBABLE TIME AND PLACE OF
PRINCIPAL EVENTS AND TEACHINGS

—IN—

The Life of Jesus of Nazareth

And their Representation by Figures and Diagrams in a Chart,
clearly indicating to the eye His Sojournings and His
Journeyings, and the Harmonized Relations of those Recorded
Times and Places, Events and Instructions, according, chiefly,
to those Authors.

———

PREFACE.

In the International series of Sunday School lessons, the New Testament Scriptures are repeatedly and frequently pursued as subjects of study.

The object of this work is to be an essential aid, both to learners and to teachers of the Gospel History. The progress of students and their success as learners, depend not more upon their application than upon their opportunities and their facilities for study. This design is both a facility and an opportunity for their progress and attainments in knowledge of New Testament Scripture. The proficiency and the effectiveness of teachers depend, not more upon their desire and their endeavor than upon their means, their helps, their utilities in teaching, and their habitual and dilligent application of them. This work is both a means of interest, and an application of means in the interest of teachers.

The design of this study is chiefly illustration—illustration, in order to facilitate the student's work, the teacher's success.

In pursuing this object, the aim and expectation has been, not to supersede the efforts and work of others, but to supplement them in a very important way—in a most effective manner, by designating events in order, by indicating their succession, by locating them relatively, and in showing their location by means of the diagram. In this way another important idea comes out clearly, the habit of the Master to make occasions or events, or even incidents, the opportunity for practical instruction.

Many years of practical work in teaching have demonstrated, to all educators of such experience, the great benefit of, if not indeed, the actual necessity for, illustration, for diagrams, for charts and maps. In preparing this outline of the historical contained in the gospels, the author has himself been greatly benefited by obtaining clearer views and more definite knowledge of the subjects considered ; and, having frequently used these diagrams in illustrating the progress of the narrative, the relation of probable times, places and principal events, and having been often assured of their helpfulness by those in his classes, and others interested in them, he confidently commends their use to the consideration of both pupils and teachers, students and instructors, as being equally adapted, available and beneficial to each, in the objects of his effort.

Being in outline only, many titles have been made as comprehensive as possible, and yet be easily and clearly understood, and at the same time be, in the main, adapted to illustration by a chart, not covering any more time than is embraced in that to accompany this key.

The distinctive features, or grounds of excellence, not heretofore utilized, so far as I know, in any of all the devices or means common in the very general, even International work of Sunday School instruction, upon which it is hoped this work will prove suggestive and helpful, are :

First, the graduated scales representing the several periods of time proportionally, the second containing all the others, the others illustrating the first.

Second, the divisions of time in the record being herein primarily and distinctively in accordance with present day custom and chronology, and the divisions of events according to these later divisions of time.

Third, the composition and expression of the title to an event, in a way clearly to suggest something definite, and whenever practicable in a way to indicate something further, and desirable to be known about it.

But the more particular intent, in the general design and the several diagrams, is to represent the whole time of that life, the three several historic periods into which it is divided, together with the unknown years, or the years of unwritten history in that life, and to do it all correctly, accurately, scientifically, and to accomplish these results, by doing it in the only way possible, by means of graduated scales, and so representing, at a single glance, the different periods of time proportionally, and the times of principal events relatively. This idea, in its application to this subject, as a whole, and in parts corresponding, is thought to be peculiar and distinctive to this design.

The result may not be all that could be wished : may not be, indeed, in many respects to your liking, but if it shall incite you to a more critical study of the subject, and help the young to clearer views of fundamental facts in the history, and stimulate and assist them and their teachers in the attainment of better results in the historical, the spiritual, the doctrinal, the ethical, the practical, than have been heretofore obtained, then will be realized, gratefully indeed, the object of the Author.

JAMES O. BLAKELEY.

The Gospels--Harmonized Account.

PRINCIPAL DIVISIONS.

OUTLINE HARMONY OF THE GOSPELS

AND

KEY TO AN OUTLINE CHART

OF

THE JOURNEYINGS, PRINCIPAL EVENTS AND

TEACHINGS IN THE LIFE OF JESUS,

THE CHRIST.

SECTION I.

INTRODUCTORY TOPICS.

1. Prefaces to Gospels.—Mark 1, 1–3; Luke 1, 1–4; John 1, 1–14.

2. The Two Genealogies.—Matt. 1, 1–17 ; Luke 3, 23–38.

3. The Annunciation to Zacharias.—Luke 1, 5–25.

4. The Annunciation to Joseph.—Matt. 1, 18–25.

5. The Annunciation to Mary.—Luke 1, 26–38.

6. Mary's Visit to Elizabeth and Mary's Song of Praise.—Luke 1, 39–56.

7. Birth of John, the Baptist, and the Song of Praise by Zacharias.—Luke 1, 57–80.

In the left hand upper spaces of the Second Diagram in the Chart are compared three Chronological Systems, with all the corresponding dates, necessary or important to the study of time, in this connection.

In the upper spaces to the right are figures showing the time of change from the Roman period to the Christian era, with the numbers of some centuries B. C. and A. D.

About 1279 or 1304 of the Roman era, one, Dionysius Exiguus, a Roman Abbot of Scythian birth, estimated that the birth of Jesus had occurred previous to those dates, by 525 or 550 years, respectively, or in the year of Rome, 754 ; and that year therefore became the first in the new era.

It is now believed that Herod died in the year of Rome 750 ; but it is not known by how many years the birth of Jesus antedates that period.

In those upper spaces to the right are also represented some important principal periods in general history, as :

1. Ancient History—All preceding A. D. 476.

2. Medieval History—From A. D. 476-A. D. 1500, more or less.

3. Modern History—All since A. D. 1500, more or less.

4. The Dark Ages—From A. D. 476-A. D. 1100.

5. The Period of Revival—From A. D. 1100-A. D. 1500, more or less.

6. The Period of Religious Reformation—From A. D. 1500 to A. D. 1650, more or less.

7. The Period of Political Revolution—Since A. D. 1650, more or less.

8. The Modern Science of Chronology, Founded A. D. 1580.

In the *third* horizontal line are numbers representing 35 years in the present system of Chronology.

In the *fourth* line, the thirty-five spaces represent thirty-five years; the first space represents the year assumed to be that of the birth of Jesus, and the other spaces the years of his age, opposite corresponding years in the present system of Chronology.

The short horizontal lines, indicated by "A," "B" and "C," represent the several and only periods of record in his life.

The intermediate spaces represent the unknown years of his life, or those of his unwritten history.

SECTION II.

HIS EARLY HISTORY.

The Short Line designated "A" represents the time of infancy, and includes events embraced in titles opposite these following numbers 8-15, as,

8. The Coming of Joseph and Mary from Nazareth to Bethlehem, and the birth of Jesus.—Luke 2, 1-7.

9. The Visit of the Shepherds to Jesus at Bethlehem.—Luke 2, 8-20.

10. The Circumcision of the Child in Bethlehem, and naming Him Jesus.—Luke 2, 21.

11. His Presentation in the Temple at Jerusalem ; Simeon's Salutation ; The Salutation of the Prophetess Anna ; The Return of the Family into Galilee and the child's growth.—Luke 2, 22-40.

12. The Coming of the Wise Men to Herod at Jerusalem ; Their Visit to Jesus at Bethlehem and their return Home, without returning to Herod. — Matt. 2, 1-12.

13. The Warning to Joseph and the Flight of Himself and Family into Egypt.—Matt. 2, 13-15.

14. The Wrath of Herod and the Havoc he Wrought in Bethlehem.—Matt. 2, 16-18.

15. Herod's Death (in the year of Rome 750) and the Going of Joseph and his Family into Galilee.—Matt. 2, 19-23.

SECTION III.

THE YOUTH OF JESUS.

The Short Line designated "B" represents *the time of One Event* in The Youth of Jesus; as,

16. His attendance at the Passover in Jerusalem at twelve years of age; His conversation with the Doctors; The return home and His continued growth and progress. —Luke 2, 41-52.

The line designated "C" represents the Three and One-Fourth years of His Public Ministry.

In the *Second* diagram are again represented the Three and One-Fourth years of his Public Ministry by Months; that is, the previous scale twelve times enlarged.

The places of the numbers along the line of journeys indicate at once both the approximate or probable time and place of events, particular events in the course being designated by the title opposite the corresponding number in the list of titles; the *time*, by the month and year directly above, and the *place* in the margin opposite, at the left.

In the last diagram, number 5, in the lower corner of the Chart, at the right, are lines representing several journeys suggested in the Scripture already considered, but not elsewhere illustrated among the journeys in the Chart; as,

1. That of Zacharias, from Hebron to Jerusalem and his return to Hebron.

2. That of Mary, from Nazareth to Hebron and her return to Nazareth.

3. That of Joseph and Mary from Nazareth to Bethlehem, to Jerusalem and their return to Nazareth.

4. That of the Shepherds.

5. That of the Wise Men.

6. That of Joseph and his family from Bethlehem to Egypt and to Nazareth.

7. That of Joseph and his family from Nazareth to Jerusalem to Passover and their return to Nazareth.

HIS PUBLIC MINISTRY.

First Year, A. D. 27—The 31st Year of His Age.

17. The Preaching and the Baptism of John at the Jordan.—Matt. 3, 1–12; Mark 1, 4–8; Luke 3, 1–18.

18. The Coming of Jesus to the Jordan and His Baptism by John.—Matt. 3, 13–17; Mark 1, 9–11; Luke 3, 21–22.

19. The Three Great Temptations.—Matt. 4, 1–11; Mark 1, 12–13; Luke 4, 1–13.

20. The First Testimony of John at the Jordan.—John 1, 15–34.

21. The First Disciples of Jesus at the Jordan.—John 1, 35–51.

22. His Attendance at a Wedding Feast at Cana; Also his First Recorded Visit to Capernaum.—John 2, 1–12.

23. He Attends the Passover Feast at Jerusalem, and Drives the Traders from the Temple—first time.—John 2, 13–25.

24. The Master instructs the Ruler, Nicodemus —John 3, 1–21.

25. The Ministry of Jesus in Judea.—John 3, 22.

26. The Second Testimony of John at the Jordan. —John 3, 23–36.

27. John's Imprisonment and the Departure of Jesus into Galilee and unto Nazareth.—Matt. 4, 12; Matt. 14, 3–5; Mark 1, 14–15; Mark 6, 17–20; Luke 3, 19–20; John 4, 1–4.

28. On the way to Galilee, Jesus teaches at Jacob's Well, near to Sychar, a city in Samaria, and many Samaritans believe on Him.—John 4, 5–42.

29. He Begins His Public Ministry in Galilee.—Mark 1, 14–15; (See 27); Luke 4, 14–15; John 4, 43–45.

30. He Heals a Nobleman's Son, He being at Cana, and the Son at Capernaum. John 4, 46–54.

Second Year, A. D. 28—The 32d Year of His Age.

31. Being offended at His preaching, the People of Nazareth reject Him. They also attempt His life. He goes to live in Capernaum.—Matt. 4, 13–17; Luke 4, 16–32.

32. He speaks from a boat on Lake Galilee; He directs a draught of fishes; He calls the Fishermen.—Matt. 4, 18–22; Mark 1, 16–20; Luke 5, 1–11.

33. He cures a Demoniac in the Synagogue at Capernaum on the Sabbath day; and the fame of Him went out into every place of the country round about.—Mark 1, 21–28; Luke 4, 33–37.

34. When they were come out of the Synagogue and into the house of Simon and Andrew, He healed Peter's wife's Mother, and others.—Matt. 8, 14–17; Mark 1, 29–34; Luke 4, 38–41.

35. He Preaches and Heals throughout all Galilee —First Circuit.—Matt. 4, 23–25; Mark 1, 35–39; Luke 4, 42–44.

36. An Instance of Healing—That of a Leper.—Matt. 8, 2–4; Mark 1, 40–44; Luke 5, 12–15.

37. Being unable to continue openly in the City, He withdrew into the wilderness across the Lake.—Mark 1, 45; Luke 5, 16.

38. Returning across the Lake and entering into Capernaum, after some days, he healed a Paralytic, borne to him of four. The Scribes and the Pharisees criticise, asking : "Why speaketh this man blasphemies?" His answer.—Matt. 9, 1-8 ; Mark 2, 1-12 ; Luke 5, 17-26.

39. Leaving the house and going forth by the Seaside, He saw Matthew and called him to follow him. —Matt. 9, 9; Mark 2, 13-14; Luke 5, 27-28.

40. The Feast by Matthew ; Many Publicans and Sinners also there, with Jesus and His Disciples; The Pharisees murmur ; He justifies Himself and reproaches them. Matt. 9, 10-13; Mark 2, 15-17 ; Luke 5, 29-32.

41. The Disciples of John also questioned Him, concerning the assumed neglect of certain ceremonies or observances on the part of His disciples ; His Answer.— Matt. 9, 14-17 ; Mark 2, 18-22 ; Luke 5, 33-39.

42. He attends the Purim? or the Passover Feast at Jerusalem; He heals an infirm man at the Pool of Bethesda on the Sabbath day ; Therefore did the Jews persecute Jesus and seek to kill him.—John 5, 1-16.

43. Jesus saying in justification of His act, " My Father worketh hitherto and I work," therefore the Jews sought the more to slay him."—John 5, 17-47.

44. Passing through the fields on the Sabbath day the Disciples pluck some grain; the Pharisees charge *violation* of the Sabbath Law ; He justifies their act by that of David and those of the Priests.—Matt. 12, 1-9 ; Mark 2, 23-28 ; Luke 6, 1-5.

45. He, Himself, healed a withered hand on the Sabbath day and being questioned by the Scribes and the Pharisees, He justified the act by their customs; Being filled with madness and having sought accusation against Him, the Pharisees took counsel with the Herodians how they might destroy Him.—Matt. 12, 10-14 ; Mark 3, 1-6 ; Luke 6, 6-11.

46. But when Jesus knew it, He withdrew himself from that place and the multitudes pressing upon him.—Matt. 12, 15–21 ; Mark 3, 7–12.

47. The Twelve Disciples Chosen.—Mark 3, 13–19; Luke 6, 12–16.

48. The Sermon on the Mount.—Matt. 5, 1–7,29 ; Luke 6, 20–49.

49. The crowds that still throng Him ; The Assertion of *Some* concerning Him ; The Desire of the *Multitude* respecting Him.—Matt. 8, 1 ; Mark 3, 20–21 ; Luke 6, 17–19.

50. A certain Centurian causes the Jewish Elders to seek Jesus, to heal his sick servant.—Matt. 8, 5–13 ; Luke 7, 1–10.

51, A Widow's Son is Restored, at Nain.—Luke 7, 11–18.

52. John sends Messengers to Jesus at Capernaum and Jesus returns messages to John at Macherus.—Matt. 11, 2–6; Luke 7, 19–23.

53. The Eulogy of Jesus upon John, to the Multitude, John's Disciples having departed.—Matt. 11, 7–19 ; Luke 7, 24–35.

54. Jesus upbraids the Unrepentant in the Cities of Chorazin, Bethsaida and Capernaum ; but encourages and assures humble followers.—Matt. 11, 20–30.

55. Feasted by a Pharisee ; Annointed by an Outcast ; Their Conduct Contrasted.—Luke 7, 36–50.

56. All the Cities and Villages of Galilee are again visited — Second Circuit.—Luke 8, 1–3.

57. He casts out a Dumb Devil ; The Pharisees accuse Him of being in league with the Prince of Devils; His Answer to them, as Vipers and Blasphemers.—Matt. 12, 22–37 ; Mark 3, 22–30 ; Luke 11, 14–26.

58. The Scribes and the Pharisees seek from Him a sign ; He refuses, pronouncing them unfaithful in the honor and use of what they already have.—Matt. 12, 38-45 ; Luke 11, 29-36.

59. His Mother and His Brethern seek Him in a crowd ; He designates His Spiritual kindred.—Matt. 12, 46-50; Mark 3, 31-35 ; Luke 8, 19-21 ; Luke 11, 27-28.

60. Dining with a certain Pharisee, the Scribes and the Pharisees began to urge Him vehemently, laying wait for Him, that they might accuse Him. He conclusively makes accusation against them, by classes.— Luke 11, 37-54.

61. He teaches an innumerable Multitude concerning the true riches, real treasure, incorruptible wealth.— Luke 12. 1-59.

62. Being told of certain Galileans who had been slain by the Governor, He assured those present, that neither they, nor certain others, who had been killed by a falling tower, were greater sinners than other Galileans; The Parable of the *unproductive* Fig Tree.—Luke 13, 1-9.

63. The Great Multitudes at the Sea-side ; The Parable of the Sower, the Tares, and other parables.— Matt. 13, 1-52 ; Mark 4, 1-35 ; Luke 8, 4-18.

64. Crossing the Lake with His Disciples into Decapolis, He stills a Tempest.—Matt. 8, 18-27 ; Mark 4, 36-41 ; Luke 8, 22-25.

65. The Demons and the Swine in the Country of the Gadarenes ; The Petition to Jesus to depart and His return across the Lake, into His own city.—Matt. 8, 28-9, 1 ; Mark 5, 1-21 ; Luke 8, 26-40.

66. Jesus Raises the Daughter of Jairus and heals another woman.—Matt. 9, 18-26 ; Mark 5, 22-43 ; Luke 8, 41-56.

67. Two Blind Men and a Dumb Man are also healed by Him. The accusation by the Pharisees.—Matt. 9, 27-34.

Third Year, A. D. 29—The 33rd Year of His Age.

68. Without Honor at Home; His Second Rejection by the People of Nazareth.—Matt. 13, 53-58; Mark 6, 1-6.

69. He again goes about all the cities and villages of Galilee — Third Circuit.—Matt. 9, 35-38.

70. The Twelve Disciples are Instructed and Sent Forth.—Matt. 10, 1-11, 1; Mark 6, 7-13; Luke 9, 1-6.

71. Herod, the King, beheads John, the Baptist.—Mat. 14, 6-11.; Mark 6, 21-29.

72. Return of the Twelve and the Departure by ship, privately into a Desert place, in Decapolis, instead of attending the Third Passover Feast of Jerusalem.—Matt. 14, 12-14. Mark 6, 30-34; Luke 9, 10-11; John 6, 1-4.

73. The Feeding of Five Thousand in Decapolis.—Matt. 14, 15-21; Mark 6, 35-44; Luke 9, 12-17; John 6, 5-14.

74. Perceiving they would take Him by force and make Him King, He departed by Himself alone into a Mountain.—Mark 6, 45-46; John 6, 15.

75. His Disciples having started across the Lake, on their return into Galilee, Jesus follows, walking upon water.—Matt. 14, 22-36; Mark 6, 47-56; John 6, 16-21.

76. Being again in Capernaum, He teaches the Multitude concerning the Bread of Life.—John 6, 22-59.

77. Considering the conditions too difficult for their continuance in the Company, many Disciples turn back and walk no more with Him.—John 6, 60-71.

78. Herod accounts for the Wonderful Works and Fame of Jesus.—Matt. 14, 1–2 ; Mark 6, 14–16 ; Luke, 9, 7–9.

79. The Scribes and the Pharisees from Jerusalem criticise and are criticised and become offended.—Matt. 15-1-20, Mark 7, 1–23.

80. Jesus departs into the Coasts of Tyre and Sidon.—Matt. 15, 21 ; Mark 7, 24.

81. He Heals the Daughter of a Syro-Phœnician Woman.—Matt. 15, 22–28; Mark 7, 25–30.

82. His return to the Eastern side of Lake Galilee; The Multitudes that came to Him and His great work of healing there.—Matt. 15, 29–31 ; Mark 7, 31–37.

83. The Feeding of Four Thousand in Decapolis.—Matt. 15, 32–38 ; Mark 8, 1–9.

84. Crossing the Lake into Galilee, He comes into the Coasts of Magdala' and Dalmanutha.—Matt. 15, 39 ; Mark 8, 10.

85. Tempting, or rather Testing Him, the Pharisees and the Sadducees unite in seeking a sign from Heaven ; He answered them that in Jonah's experience and their own were to be found the only infallible signs vouchsafed by Heaven.—Matt. 16, 1–4 ; Mark 8, 11–12.

86. Leaving them at once and recrossing the Lake into Decapolis, He charged His Disciples to beware of the leaven of the Pharisees, the Sadducees and Herod.—Matt. 16, 5–12 ; Mark 8, 13–21.

87. At Bethsaida a Blind Man, partially healed, sees Men as trees walking.—Mark 8, 22–26.

88. Being in the vicinity of Cesarea Philippi, He asks and hears various opinions concerning himself.—Matt, 16, 13–20; Mark 8, 27–30 ; Luke 9, 18–20.

89. His First Prediction of His Death and Resurrection.—Matt. 16, 21–28 ; Mark 8, 31–9, 1; Luke 9, 21–27.

90. Being in a High Mountain with Peter, James and John, Jesus is Transfigured before them.—Matt. 17, 1–13 ; Mark 9, 2–13 ; Luke 9, 28–36.

91. Coming Back to the Multitude, a Lunatic, unhealed by the Disciples is restored by the Master.—Matt. 17, 14–21 ; Mark 9, 14–29; Luke 9, 37–42.

92. Returning into Galilee He makes the Second, Prediction of His Death and Resurrection.—Matt. 17, 22–23; Mark 9, 30–32 ; Luke 9, 43–45.

93. At Capernaum, the Tribute Money or Temple tax is Sought and Received.—Matt. 17, 24–27. ·

94. His Disciples, having disputed among themselves, by the way, "Who should be greatest", He took occasion to teach them concerning the wisdom of humility, the importance of preventing offenses, the necessity for forgiveness, charity and concord.—Matt. 18, 1–35; Mark 9, 33–50; Luke 9, 46–50.

95. His relatives assume to desire His company to the Feast of Tabernacles at Jerusalem and to wish some sort of a demonstration by Him ; He sends them on openly, Himself *following*, as it were, in secret.—John 7, 2–10.

96. Coming into the Temple about the middle of the Feast, and beginning at once to teach, some said, " Lo, He speaketh boldly and they say nothing unto him."—John 7, 11–27.

97. Afterward the Pharisees and the Chief Priests sent Officers to take Him ; why they sent, and why He was not taken.—John 7, 28–52.

98. And every man went unto his own house and Jesus unto the Mount of Olives.—John 7, 53–8, 1.

99. Being in the Temple again, next day, All the people came unto Him and He sat down and taught them ; Meanwhile, the Scribes and the Pharisees combine in a brazen and shameless effort, tempting Him, that they might have accusation against Him.—John 8, 2–11.

100. Discoursing farther and respecting The Light of the World, Spiritual Truth and Spiritual Freedom, Sonship and Service, Righteousness and Liberty, He said, "Before Abraham was, I am." Then took they up stones to cast at Him.—John 8, 12-59.

101. But Jesus hid Himself and went out of the Temple, going into Galilee and the Coasts of Judea beyond. Jordan.—Matt. 19, 1-2 ; Mark 10, 1 ; John 7, 1 and 8, 59.

102. There great Multitudes are Taught and Healed by Him.—Matt. 19, 1-2 ; Mark 10, 1.

103. At length the Feast of Dedication approaching, He steadfastly sets His face to go again to Jerusalem. —Luke 9, 51.

104. On the way, Entertainment being refused by the Samaritans, Punishment by Fire is proposed by the Disciples.—Luke 9, 52-56.

105. To the three, who would follow Him, He states frankly the nature of the undertaking, the conditions of His life, and gives warning of the sacrifices necessary to real Disciplesphip—Luke 9, 57-62.

106. The Seventy Missionaries sent out.—Luke 10, 1-16.

107. The seventy Return.—Luke 10, 17-24.

108. The Lawyer who would tempt or test Jesus, hears His gospel, in the story of the Good Samaritan.— Luke 10, 25-37.

109. Martha and Mary entertain Him at Bethany. —Luke 10, 38-42.

110. The Great Contention in the Temple, at the Feast of Dedication, about a Blind Man Healed.—John 9. 1-41.

111. False and True Shepherds ; Conflicting Opinions Concerning Jesus.—John 10, 1-21.

112. Being in Solomon's Porch, in the Temple, some say unto Jesus, "If Thou be the Christ, tell us plainly"; Jesus having replied, then they took up stones again to stone Him.—John 10, 22-31.

113. Delaying action, they charge Him with Blasphemy; Having answered them, therefore they sought again to take Him.—John 10, 32-39.

114. But He escaped out of their hand and went away again, beyond Jordan, and abode there, many resorting unto Him, and many believing on Him there.—John 10, 39-42.

Fourth Year, A. D. 30—The 34th Year of His Age

115. Being requested by His Disciples He teaches them to pray, specifying both the spirit of prayer, and of its acceptance, with illustrations of each.— Luke 11, 1-13.

116. On the Sabbath Day, He heals an infirmity of 18 years; A Synagogue Ruler's indignation; his Hypocrisy made plain.—Luke 13, 10-17.

117. Again journeying toward Jerusalem, and teaching in the cities and villages as He went, He used as illustrations, The Mustard Seed, the Leaven, the Strait gate.—Luke 13, 18-30.

118. Being told by Pharisees that Herod would kill Him, He said, "It cannot be, that a Prophet perish out of Jerusalem. O, Jerusalem! Jerusalem!"— Luke, 13, 31-35.

119. Dining with a certain Pharisee and being watched, Jesus cured a case of dropsy on the Sabbath day and justified His act by their customs.—Luke 14, 1-6.

120. Noting the strife for chief rooms at the feast, Jesus taught concerning Choice of Places, Inviting Company, Selecting Guests, Making Excuses, Sacrifices in Discipleship, Counting the Cost, and Salt with Savor in it.—Luke 14, 7-35.

121. The Publicans and Sinners drawing near to hear him, the Pharisees and the Scribes murmur; He replies, using the Parables of the Stray Sheep, the Lost Coin, the Prodigal Son.—Luke 15, 1--32.

122. He also teaches referring to an Unjust Steward; also to an attempt to serve successfully Two Masters; also respecting a Rich Man and a Beggar.—Luke 16, 1-31.

123. He adds further instructions concerning Offenses, Forgiveness, and Acceptable Service.— Luke 17, 1-10.

124. Jesus goes from Perea to Bethany and raises Lazarus.—John 11, 1-46.

125. The Chief Priests and the Pharisees from that day forth took counsel to put Him to Death.—John 11, 47-53.

126. Jesus therefore went thence into a country near to a Wilderness, into a city called Ephraim.—John 11, 54.

127. And having extended His journey into Galilee, and being in retirement, until about the time of the Fourth Passover, He again set out for Jerusalem, passing through Samaria. —Luke 17, 11.

128. He Heals Ten Lepers ; Only the Stranger, a Samaritan, returns to make acknowledgments.—Luke 17, 12-19.

129. The Pharisees demanding *When* the Kingdom of God should come, were told that it cometh not with observation or with unusual signs.—Luke 17, 20-37.

SECTION V.

THE LAST TEN DAYS.

In the Third Diagram, the last ten days are represented by one-fourth days—that is, the previous scale one hundred and twenty times enlarged.

Friday, March 31, A. D. 30.

140. On His way from Jericho, Jesus arrives at Bethany, His apprehension having been already determined by the Chief Priests and the Pharisees.—Luke 19, 28 ; John 11, 55–12, 1.

Saturday, April 1—A Memorial Day.

141. The Supper by Martha and the Annointing by Mary.—John 12, 2–9.

142. And because many believed on Jesus by reason of Lazarus, the Chief Priests consulted that they might put Lazarus also to death.—John 12, 10–11.

Sunday, April 2—Palm Sunday or Procession Day.

143. In Preparation the Disciples did as Jesus commanded them, at Bethphage, securing in the next village an unridden animal for His use that day.—Matt. 21, 1–6 ; Mark 11, 1–6 ; Luke 19, 29–35.

144. His Public Entry into Jerusalem : The Demonstration by His Friends.—Matt. 21, 7–11 ; Mark 11, 7–10 ; Luke 19, 36–38 ; John 12, 12–18.

145. The Pharisees say unto Him : " Master, rebuke Thy Disciples." His reason for declining.—Luke 19, 39–40.

146. Among themselves the Pharisees concede the world to have gone after Him and lament their inefficiency in preventing it.—John 12, 19.

147. At Eventide, having looked aronnd upon all things, He returned, with the twelve, to Bethany.—Mark 11, 11.

Monday, April 3—Expulsion Day.

148. On the way to the Temple, in the morning, occurred the incident of the Fig Tree, having on it only leaves.—Matt. 21, 18-19; Mark 11, 12-14.

149. Approaching the city He wept over it, predicting its destruction, not knowing the time of its visitation. Luke 19, 41-44.

150. Entering the Temple, the traders were expelled from it the second time.—Matt. 21, 12-13; Mark 11, 15-16; Luke 19, 45.

151. The Blind and the Lame are healed in the Temple : The Children give Him their tribute of Praise : The Chief Priests and the Scribes are sore displeased.—Matt. 21, 14-16.

152. The Scribes and the Pharisees hearing Jesus say, they had made the Temple a *den* of thieves, sought how they might destroy Him : but they feared the people. —Mark 11, 17-18; Luke 19, 46-48.

153. Leaving them and the city He went out to Bethany and lodged there.—Matt. 21, 17 . Mark 11, 19.

Tuesday, April 4—Discussion Day.

154. On the way to the Temple, in the morning, a withered Fig Tree furnished occasion for a lesson on Faith and its Fruits.—Matt. 21, 20-22 ; Mark 11, 20-26.

155. In the Temple, the Chief Priests and the Scribes and the Elders ask His authority for what He does ; He answers, by asking them concerning the Baptism of John. —Matt. 21, 23-27 ; Mark 11, 27-33 ; Luke 20, 1-8.

156. He then teaches those Authorities, conveying His instruction in three parables—The Two Sons, The Wicked Husbandmen, The marriage of the King's Son. —Matt. 21, 28-22, 14 ; Mark 12, 1-12 ; Luke 20, 9-18.

157. The Chief Priests and the Scribes, perceiving that He had spoken against them, sent spies, feigning themselves just men, so they might deliver Him unto the power and authority of the Governor.—Luke 20, 19-20.

158. Their Three Great Tests :

a—Concerning the Tribute—Political Economy.

b—Concerning the Resurrection— Speculative Theology.

c—Concerning the *Great* Commandment—Practical Religion.—Matt. 22, 15-40 ; Mark 12, 13-34 ; Luke 20, 21-40.

159. He then questioned them concerning the Christ and David, and they were unable to answer Him a word ; and from that day forth no man dared ask Him any more questions.—Matt. 22, 41-46 ; Mark 12, 35-37 ; Luke 20, 41-44.

160. Jesus warns both the multitude and His disciples against the Scribes and the Pharisees.—Matt. 23, 1-12 ; Mark 12, 38-40 ; Luke 20, 45-47.

161. Their characters are then critically and comprehensively designated and both they and their customs severely denounced.—Matt. 23, 13-33.

162. He plainly portrays the condition of Jerusalem and deeply laments it.—Matt. 23, 34-39. ,

163. He contrasts the contributions to the Temple treasury ; the Widow, giving two mites, is commended, above all the others.—Mark 12, 41-44 ; Luke 21, 1-4.

164. Some Greeks seeking Jesus are told both the nature and the conditions of acceptable service.—John 12, 20-36.

165. Fear of the Pharisees prevents open confession on the part of many who believe on Him.—John 12, 37-50.

166. Departing from the Temple (Tuesday P. M.?) His disciples call His attention to the Temple buildings, and He predicts their utter destruction.—Matt. 24, 1-2 ; Mark 13, 1-2 ; Luke 21, 5-6.

167. Being upon the Mount of Olives His Disciples ask Him privately, "When shall these things be, and what shall be the sign of Thy coming "? His answer.— Matt. 24, 3-51 ; Mark 13, 3-37; Luke 21, 7-36.

168. Further instruction is communicated by reference to the Ten Virgins ; The Bestowment of Talents ; The relation of acts to life ; and the criterion and the conditions of judgment.—Matt. 25, 1-46.

How and Where the Master's Time was occupied.— Luke 21, 37-38.

169. On Tuesday evening ?, Jesus tells His disciples that He is to be betrayed and crucified ; at the same time the Chief Priests, the Scribes and the Elders consult to take Him by subtilty and kill him.—Matt. 26, 1-5 ; Mark 14, 1-2 ; Luke 22, 1-2.

Wednesday, April 5—A Memorial Day.

170. The annointing of Jesus by a woman in the house of Simon, the Leper.—Matt. 26,6 -13 ; Mark 14, 3-9.

171. The conspiracy both to obtain and to deliver Jesus, by the Jewish Council and the Betrayer Judas.— Matt. 26, 14-16 ; Mark 14, 10-11 ; Luke 22, 3-6.

Thursday, April 6—Passover Feast Day.

172. Preparation for the Paschal Supper in Jerusalem. Securing the Guest Chamber by Disciples.—Matt. 26, 17-19; Mark 14, 12-16 ; Luke 22, 7-13.

173. The Beginning of the Feast and the expression of the Master's strong desire to eat that Passover with His Disciples, before he should suffer.—Matt. 26, 20; Mark 14, 17; Luke 22, 14-18.

174. The old strife among His disciples renewed; Who shall be accounted greatest, again in controversy.—Luke 22, 24-30.

175. An Object Lesson—To His several discourses concerning the necessity of humility and the dignity of service, Jesus now added a practical illustration and a personal example, as an ideal in those respects.—John 13, 1-20.

176. Jesus openly announces the contemplated betrayal by Judas and he withdraws from the feast and the company.—Matt. 26, 21-25; Mark 14, 18-21; Luke 22, 21-23; John 13, 21-30.

177. The Passover Feast being finished, a Memorial Service or the Lord's Supper was instituted. —Mat. 26, 26-29; Mark 14, 22-25; Luke 22, 19-20.

178. The Prediction of Peter's Three Denials.—Matt. 26, 31-35; Mark 14. 27-31; Luke 22, 31-38; John 13, 31-38.

179. The Farewell Discourse and the Intercessory Prayer.—John 14, 1-17, 26.

180. From the Guest Chamber to the Mount of Olives.—Matt. 26, 30; Mark 14, 26; Luke 22, 39; John 18, 1-2.

181. The Scene in the Garden of Gethsemane, on or near the Mount of Olives.—Matt. 26, 36-46; Mark 14, 32-42; Luke 22, 40-46.

182. Judas, coming with a band of men and officers from the Chief Priests and the Scribes and the Elders accomplishes the Betrayal; and about midnight (?) Jesus is arrested, bound and led away, first to Annas—Father-in-law to the High Priest.—Matt. 26, 47-58; Mark 14, 43-54; Luke 22, 47-54; John 18, 3-14.

183. Before day-break Annas sends Jesus bound to Caiaphas, the High Priest—that year. The Hearing, the Contempt, and the violence before him—Luke 22, 63–65; John 18, 19–24.

184. The Three Denials by Peter, before Daybreak, in the Court to Palace of High Priest.—Matt. 26, 69–75; Mark 14, 66–72; Luke 22, 55–62; John 18, 15–18; John 18, 25–27.

185. Jesus before the Jewish Council; Its Early Session; Its Brief Hearing; Its swift condemnation; The contempt and the violence in its presence.—Matt. 26, 59–68; Mark 14, 55–65; Luke 22, 66–71. Compare this order with that in John 18, 28.

186. The Compunction, the Repentance, the Confession, the Restoration, the Disdain, the Anguish and the Suicide of Judas.—Matt. 27, 3–10.

187. The hearing before Pilate; His first attempt to release Jesus; He at length, sends Him to Herod.—Matt. 27, 1–2; Matt. 27, 11–14; Mark 15, 1–5; Luke 23, 1–7; John 18, 28–38.

188. Herod questions Jesus in many words, sets Him at naught, arrays Him in a gorgeous robe, mocks Him and returns Him to Pilate.—Luke 23, 8–12.

189. Pilate knowing that for envy Jesus had been delivered to him, again seeks his release; But the Chief Priests and the Elders persuaded the multitude to ask Barabbas instead and destroy Jesus. Matt. 27, 15–25; Mark 15, 6–14; Luke 23, 13–23; John 18, 39–40.

190. Pilate releases the robber Barabbas and delivers Jesus to the soldiers to be scourged; the Cruelty, the Contempt, and the Mocking of the Soldiers at the scourging.–Matt. 27, 26–31; Mark 15, 15–20; John 19, 1–3.

191. Pilate's Third Attempt to Release Jesus ; But the Chief Priests and Officers continue to demand the death sentence upon him.—John 19, 4–12.

192. Position finally compels Pilate's surrender and Jesus is delivered and led away to be crucified.—Luke 23, 24–25 ; John 19, 12–16.

193. The Cyrenian, the great company of People and of women and the two malefactors on the way to Calvary.—Matt. 27, 32–34 ; Mark 15, 21–23 ; Luke 23, 26–32 ; John 19, 17–18.

194. The Crucifixion ; the Inscription and Casting Lots.—Matt. 27, 35–38 ; Mark 15, 24–28 ; Luke 23, 33–34 and 38 ; John 19, 19–24.

195. The Mockery at the Cross by those passing, by the Robbers, the Soldiers, the Rulers, the Elders and the Chief Priests.—Matt. 27, 39–49 ; Mark 15, 29–36 ; Luke 28, 35–37 ; Luke 23, 39–45.

196. The Women at the Cross ; Jesus, his mother and John.—Matt. 27, 55–56 ; Mark 15, 40–41 : Luke 23, 48–49 ; John 19, 25–27.

197. The Crowning Act of Wickedness is consummated ; a Life of Sacrifice is closed by the Great Sacrifice, the Death of Jesus on the Cross.—Matt. 27, 50–53 ; Mark 15, 37–38 ; Luke 23, 46 ; John 19, 28–37.

198. The Centurian's Testimony.—Matt. 27, 54 ; Mark 15, 39 ; Luke 23, 47.

199. The Burial in the New Tomb of Joseph.—Matt. 27, 57–61 ; Mark 15, 42–47 ; Luke 23, 50–56 ; John 19, 38–42.

Saturday, April 8 — Sorrow's Day and Security.

200. The Sepulcher Guarded by the Soldiers.—Matt. 27, 62–66.

Sunday, April 9—Resurrection Day.

201. The Gospel of the Resurrection is communicated to the women first at the sepulcher.—Matt. 23, 1–10 ; Mark 16, 1–9 ; Luke 24, 1–7 ; John 20, 1–17.

202. The Chief Priest and the Elders — and the Guards' Report.—Matt. 23, 11–15.

203. The Disciples receive Knowledge and Experience of the Resurrection, and Proclaim it to the World —Matt. 28, 16–20 ; Mark 16, 10–20 ; Luke 24, 8–53 ; John 20, 18–21, 25.

In Him was life ; and that life was the light of men.—*John 1: 4.*

He that followeth me shall not walk in darkness, but have the light of life.—*John 8: 12.*

www.ingramcontent.com/pod-product-compliance
Lightning Source LLC
Chambersburg PA
CBHW021457090426
42739CB00009B/1762